TH]
THAT
MOST

MARK FINLEY and STEVEN MOSLEY

Pacific Press® Publishing Association

Nampa, Idaho

Oshawa, Ontario, Canada

Edited by Kenneth R. Wade
Cover by Center Graphics

Copyright © 1997 by
Pacific Press® Publishing Association
Printed in the United States of America
All rights reserved

Finley, Mark, 1945-
   Things that matter most / Mark Finley and Steven
Mosley.
      p.   cm.
   ISBN 0-8163-1584-1 (alk. paper)
   1. Christian life—Seventh-day Adventist authors. I.
Mosley, Steven R., 1952- . II. Title.
BV4501.2.F483 1998
248.4'86732—dc21   98-9321
                                                        CIP

98 99 00 01 • 5 4 3 2

Contents

Introduction

What matters most in your life? What drives you? What pushes you to work extra hours? Is it money? Prestige? Power? Job security? Or is it possibly pleasure—your boat, sports, or a fascination with gambling? What really matters most in your life? In a recent survey, when people were asked what really mattered in their lives, they mentioned God, family, their health, security, and peace of mind. But when their lifestyle practices were compared to the priorities they listed, the two were vastly different.

In this volume, *Things That Matter Most*, we are going to look at the things that really count in life. Steve and I are concerned about the things that will endure. Some things are temporary. They evaporate like the dew on a spring morning. They fade away like foggy mists before the rising sun. Other things last forever—they endure.

We will delve into the physical, the mental, the social, and the spiritual aspects of life. We'll discover how to have an effective prayer life, why Bible study transforms your life, and how to make Bible study interesting. Steve and I will give you pointers on how to enhance your physical health. You will rediscover the value of a good diet and adequate exercise as well as receiving some practical tips on how to apply these health principles to your life.

We will also discuss how to resolve conflict, how to enhance interpersonal relationships, and how to build a secure, happy future with the people around you.

Things That Matter Most can make a difference in your life. It presents much more than surface solutions to complex problems. The principles that we outline here work. I've seen tens of thousands of people's lives changed as they have applied them. This book is designed not only to be read, but its principles are designed to be put into practice in your life.

As Jesus said 2000 years ago, "Happy are you if you know these things and do them" (John 13:17). Steve and I wish you a life filled with abundant happiness as you place your priority on "the things that matter most."

Mark A. Finley

Wired for God

Human beings have been looking for God since the world began. They've climbed the highest mountains in search of Him, gone on long pilgrimages to reach Him. They've peered into distant galaxies for traces of His power. People have looked for God in a wide variety of mystical experiences and sacred writings.

But new evidence indicates we may find God's fingerprints very close to home, closer than we've imagined. It appears that God has a specific place in our minds—because of the way that our brains are wired.

Why does faith make people healthier? A few years ago scientists finally began to try to answer that question. And that's what led to new discoveries about how our brains are wired.

The evidence about faith and health has been accumulating for some time. In 1995, the Dartmouth-Hitchcock Medical Center conducted a study of heart-surgery patients. They found that the best predictor of survival was—the degree to which these patients drew strength and comfort from religious faith. Those who didn't have such faith were three times more likely to die.

Other research has demonstrated that churchgoers have lower blood pressure than non-churchgoers, and they have half the risk of dying from coronary-artery disease.

And these studies were adjusted to account for smoking and other risk factors.

In other words, let's compare smokers who value religion as important with smokers that don't. What do we find? The religious individuals are one-seventh as likely to have abnormal blood pressure.

Now, don't misunderstand me, I'm not suggesting that you go out and start puffing away, not at all. If you're religious and you don't smoke, you're likely to have lower blood pressure than if you're religious and you do smoke.

But some people, looking over these new findings might conclude: "Well, maybe it's just the social aspect of our churchgoing. Maybe it's just being with other people that produces such positive effects on our health."

But, one heart-surgery study isolated this factor; it studied how much individuals drew comfort from faith and how much they participated in social groups. The results? Both of these factors appear to have distinct benefits, and they make a powerful combination.

Time magazine reports, "Those who were *both* religious and socially involved had a fourteenfold advantage over those who were isolated or lacked faith."

Fourteen times healthier? That's pretty significant.

It's no wonder scientists began looking at why faith makes people healthier.

In 1975, a Harvard physician named Herbert Benson wrote a bestseller *The Relaxation Response*. He had developed a simple technique to help people reduce stress. He helped them focus their minds on a single word or image and completely relax their bodies. People could reduce their heart rate, their respiration and stress-related hormones.

Dr. Benson was able to help people who couldn't sleep well, insomniacs, and those suffering from chronic pain. The "Relaxation Response" even helped some infertile women to conceive.

And then Dr. Benson began to notice something especially interesting. There was a certain sub-group of patients who benefited from the "relaxation response" more than others. They had even better health, even more rapid recoveries. Who were they? People who said they felt a sense of closeness to God while meditating. They were doing more than just relaxing. They felt the intimate presence of the God of the universe. And this produced the most powerful results.

Dr. Benson began to study exactly what was happening to these people when they experienced this closeness to God. He, along with others, studied the brain; they studied the way the brain is wired; they studied the way different parts of the brain react when stimulated. And these scientists managed to pinpoint the headquarters of religious experience in the brain—it's a small, almond-shaped structure called the amygdala.

The amygdala, along with the hippocampus and hypothalamus, makes up the limbic system of the brain. The limbic system controls emotions, sexual pleasure, deepfelt memories and, it appears, spirituality.

This is what scientists have found. When the amygdala, or the hippocampus, is electrically stimulated during surgery, some patients have visions of angels or demons. Scientists have also looked at people whose limbic systems are overstimulated by drug abuse or a tumor. They found that these individuals often become religious fanatics.

As a result of these discoveries, neuroscientist Rhawn Joseph had to conclude: "The ability to have religious experiences has a neuroanatomical basis." What was he saying? He's saying, We've got religion in our heads.

Dr. Herbert Benson puts it even more strongly. In his latest book, *Timeless Healing,* he writes this: "Our genetic blueprint has made believing in an Infinite, an absolute part of our nature." The doctor goes on to say, "We're wired for God."

Wired for God. This isn't coming out of devotional, religious literature. This isn't something someone thought up in a mystical moment on a mountaintop. This is what the scientists are saying. They know about faith and health now. They know that faith really *does* something to us. They know more about the brain now. They know about what different areas of the brain do. They've pinpointed the amygdala in the limbic system.

And the bottom line is this—we are wired for God.

Listen to how this fact was expressed long ago by David in Psalm 139. In his praise of the Creator, the psalmist says, describing the way our bodies were created: "For you created my inmost being; you knit me together in my mother's womb. I praise you because I am fearfully and wonderfully made . . ." (Psalm 139:13, 14, NIV).

Fearfully and wonderfully made. Our discoveries about the amygdala give new meaning to that phrase, "fearfully and wonderfully made." Yes, God created our inmost being. Of course, He's reserved a special place for Himself in our neurological wiring. That's what you'd expect a loving Creator who wants a relationship with us to do.

The prophet Zechariah described our Creator in this way: "the Lord, who . . . forms the spirit of man within him" (Zechariah 12:1, NKJV).

God has formed the spirit deep within us, the soul deep within us. He's given it a special shape. We're not just the product of animal instincts. We're wired for more than just survival of the fittest, friend. God has created us as spiritual beings. He's made us for Himself.

Look at these words from another psalm. The Bible makes it plain, we're wired for God, we're made for God, we're created for God. The scripture says: "Know that the Lord is God. It is he who made us, and we are his; we are his people, the sheep of his pasture" (Psalm 100:3, NIV).

We are His. God made us. We belong to Him. We were made to follow Him like sheep following a shepherd to green pastures and still waters. And the wonderful fact is this: God has given us the ability to know Him, the desire to know Him, the longing to know Him. It's in the very way that our brains are wired. It's a part of our limbic system.

That's the good news. There's also some sad news.

As human beings, we don't always pay attention to the way we're wired. Unfortunately, we don't always listen to that still, small voice. We don't always respond to the heart that says, "Seek God's face."

We're wired for God. But we can become unwired, rewired, or cross-wired. We can get our priorities all mixed up.

In the first three chapters of the book of Romans, Paul lays out the tragedy of our human condition. And this is how he sums it up—powerful passages that describe how human beings can fall from the state that God created them in, how their brains can actually become rewired.

The Scripture says: "although they knew God, they did not glorify Him as God . . . Professing to be wise, they became fools, who exchanged the truth of God for the lie . . . as they did not like to retain God in their knowledge, God gave them over to a debased mind . . ." (Romans 1:21, 22, 25, 28 , NKJV).

There you have it, God has placed the knowledge of Himself within us. But our minds can become debased. We can rewire our brains with lies.

This is the warning that God gave to a certain generation that had turned its back on Him. The Bible says: "My spirit shall not strive with man forever . . ."(Genesis 6:3, NKJV).

That spirit, that spiritual nature that is a gift from God, can tragically be lost.

The truth that God has woven into our minds can disappear. We can ignore it. We can repress it. We can pervert it. We can short-circuit the wisdom that God gives us.

Take a certain unfortunate minister in Nashville, for example. He started playing electronic poker down at the local arcade. It was just a pastime at first, just something to help him relax. But it turned into a compulsion. He couldn't stop playing. He couldn't stop spending his money.

This pastor had done a pretty good job at his church. He had never scandalized his congregation. But now, the poker compulsion just took over. Nothing was more important. His brain had been rewired. The man had to quit pastoring, and he went to work as a janitor. But he needed more money to support his addiction. Finally, he committed armed robbery.

Human beings are fragile. Our wiring gets messed up. We can be overwhelmed by compulsions. People lose sight of what matters most.

We invest everything in getting ahead financially. And then wake up one morning—shocked by how empty our lives have become.

We invest everything in building a dream house. And then wake up one morning—shocked by how cold our home has become.

We get wound up, stressed out and hemmed in by all kinds of things. We're on the fast track. But we keep missing our destination. We keep passing by the things that matter most.

We're trying to focus on what we really need as human beings, what we can't live without.

And it's a good idea to start with who we are, what we're made for. Poetically speaking, we can talk about the shape of our hearts. Scientifically speaking, we can talk about how our brains are wired.

But the bottom line is that we need to center our lives on God in order to be healthy. There's no way to get around that. And that's how we're wired.

In the mid-60s, Noel Paul Stookey made it to the top of the pop music business. He was performing 150 nights a year with America's most beloved folk group, Peter, Paul and Mary.

Limousines waited for him at every airport. Enthusiastic

fans crammed every concert hall. He could wake up in expensive hotels to a breakfast of champagne and strawberries.

But in all this fast-paced, first-class lifestyle, something was missing. Behind his successful image he felt terribly empty. All the praise bothered him. He was cut off from contact with real people. He hardly knew his own wife and child.

Noel began to see himself as a papier-mâché person, very expensively decked out on the surface, but hollow and held together by thin glue. He kept asking himself, "Is life nothing more than a great scramble for advantage? What is all this for?"

He started looking for answers. He read the Tibetan Book of the Dead. He read books by the spiritualist Edgar Cayce.

That little almond-shaped part of Noel's mind was compelling him to search. At the time, he didn't believe it was really possible to know God. But something kept him looking.

And finally, most unexpectedly, this singer found his answer. It was just a conversation, a casual conversation, in a hotel room, just a young man who wanted to talk after a concert. But this Christian believer encouraged Noel to pray, to talk directly to God.

And that broke something open inside of him. Noel began to weep. And all he could say was, "I'm sorry." He was sorry that he'd let things get between himself and other people. He was sorry he'd ignored God for so long.

At last Noel Stookey knew exactly what mattered most. Suddenly, he understood what he'd been made for. This is how he recalled the experience, "Suddenly, when I had admitted that I was sorry for the life I had led without God, everything collapsed, and I was perfectly balanced. I had been given day one again."

After this encounter with God, prayer became vital for Noel. He began devouring the Bible. He kept meeting believers everywhere he went. And he decided to make a new commitment to his family.

Noel Stookey had discovered the right starting point. All the success he'd experienced, all the fame that had come his way, didn't really add up to much without this one thing, his relationship with God. That's what he'd been made for. That's what mattered most. That's how his brain was now wired.

Noel described his new, happier, more centered life in this way: "Before I was a Christian, I performed to entertain and to be entertained. I derived a lot of satisfaction out of performing. I still do. But now the satisfaction is similar to what you get from doing a favor or a kindness for someone. I feel that I'm of service to the people in my audience."

This singer's discovery about what matters most in life reminds me of another man who'd reached the top in his world. A brilliant young Pharisee named Saul had made it to the top—intellectually and socially—in Jewish society. But then he met an Individual who made all his achievements seem insignificant in comparison.

Saul, as the apostle Paul, wrote these words to express what he'd found. "But whatever was to my profit I now consider loss for the sake of Christ. What is more, I consider everything a loss compared to the surpassing greatness of knowing Christ Jesus my Lord, for whose sake I have lost all things. I consider them rubbish, that I may gain Christ . . ." (Philippians 3:7, 8, NIV).

After his conversion, Paul was banished from the elite circles in which he'd made his mark. He lost his position. He lost his prestige. And he'd gained only one thing—Jesus Christ.

But that relationship weighed more to him in the balance than the whole world. He was experiencing the "surpassing greatness" of knowing Christ. Like Noel Stookey, he found himself perfectly balanced. He'd been given day one again.

Why? Because he was created for that relationship. His brain was wired for that relationship. He could finally say, "This is what it means to truly be alive!" That's what he wrote to the Philippians. He put it very simply, very profoundly in Philippians: "For to me, to live is Christ . . ." (Philippians 1:21, NIV).

Friends, there are consolations in this life if you don't become company president. There are consolations if you don't become a millionaire. There are consolations if you never build your dream house. You can find other pleasures, other sources of satisfaction.

But there is no consolation if you don't find God. There's no consolation if you don't discover what matters most.

We can stay busy, we can keep pursuing things our whole life, and neglect what's most important. We can ignore and repress the longing in our hearts, the message wired into our brains. And then we discover—too late—that we've missed out on everything! All the stuff we've accumulated means so little. And there's this big hole in our lives.

Don't let that happen to you. Don't wait until you're numbed. Don't wait until you're callused. Don't wait until it's too late!

There's no consolation if you don't find God. Something's missing that can't be replaced. There's no substitute; nothing else will do.

You were created to experience the "surpassing greatness" of knowing Christ. It's right there in your brain. The need is there. The longing is there. Listen to that quiet voice. Listen to God's Spirit working inside of you. Listen, please, to what matters most.

You can begin the most wonderful relationship in this world right now. You can start getting to know the one individual who makes all other achievements seem insignificant by comparison. It all begins with one step—opening up your heart to God, talking directly to God. The One who made you is waiting for your response. Why not open your heart to Him right now.

When More Becomes Less

The United States, at the head of a coalition of countries, managed to expel Saddam Hussein's troops from Kuwait during four memorable days in 1991. Lightning airstrikes from aircraft carriers, smart bombs, armored units racing across the desert—it was quite a display of military might.

And Coalition forces suffered amazingly light casualties during "Desert Storm." In fact, many of those actually were the result of "friendly fire"—forces on the same side mistakenly firing at each other.

Recent studies have revealed the common factor behind these cases of "friendly fire." It's an important issue, because it points out the price that we're paying as a 24-hour-a-day society.

Dr. Gregory Belenky wanted to know why Coalition soldiers had fired on friendly forces during Desert Storm. Battle conditions are nerve-racking and intensely chaotic—bullets zipping through the air, shells exploding all around you. It's not always easy to differentiate friends from the enemy in the heat of conflict.

Desert Storm, however, was different from most wars. Coalition forces were usually striking an enemy that lay miles away. Smart bombs zeroed in on specific targets.

American soldiers generally rolled over Iraqi positions. There was very little hand-to-hand fighting. The demoralized Iraqis often surrendered en masse.

And yet, incidents of "friendly fire" persisted. Dr. Belenky wanted to know why. And he wanted to isolate the factors that contributed to these tragic mistakes. Maybe there was something he could find out that would reduce such incidents in the future.

Dr. Belenky is a physician who works at Walter Reed Army Institute of Research. He had the facilities to study soldiers who were involved in shooting at their own troops.

And he began to isolate one common factor. All these men had one thing in common—fatigue, lack of sleep. Many had been awake for three days.

Dr. Belenky decided to find out precisely what happens to a person who is deprived of sleep for seventy-two hours. He conducted various tests. And this is what he found.

Sleep-deprived men can still march like soldiers. They can still aim their weapons like soldiers. And what's more, they can still hit the target about as well as they could before—even though it takes them a bit longer.

So, on the surface, soldiers who'd been going steadily for three days could still function physically.

But mentally something had happened. A soldier awake for seventy-two hours has trouble identifying who he is, what unit he belongs to. And he doesn't really grasp what he's firing at.

Dr. Belenky also studied the effects of sleep deprivation on Army Rangers. During their tough training campaign, they average three-and-a-half hours of sleep a night. But they have to keep going, keep pushing onward.

As a result, the Rangers experience what is called "droning." They can put one foot in front of the other. They can respond to direct commands. But they have a hard time grasping their situation. It's very difficult for them to act on their own initiative.

A lack of sleep breaks down certain mental processes. We can appear to be functioning normally, but we're not really all there.

Fatigued people can still see, for example. There's nothing wrong with their eyesight or their vision. But the brain has a hard time interpreting the visual input. It can't handle it all, so it dumps some of the information, doesn't store it. A sleep-deprived driver who causes an accident can honestly say he didn't see the car he pulled out in front of.

Sleep-deprived soldiers can still aim. They can still fire. They can still hit the target. But one very significant thing has changed. They don't know who the enemy is.

People without adequate sleep don't know who the enemy is. I think that's pretty significant for the way we live our everyday lives.

The U.S. National Institute of Health brought together a symposium in 1994. They wanted to study the effects of fatigue. The position paper that resulted is called "Wake Up America: A National Sleep Alert."

The paper documents the fact that many Americans are functionally handicapped—because of fatigue. We're just not getting enough sleep. Our work suffers, and our relationships suffer, as a result.

Since 1969, Americans have added 158 hours to their annual working/commuting time. We have less time for rest—and it really shows.

Every year, 5,000 Americans die in sleep-related accidents—thousands are injured. Billions of dollars are spent in hospital costs, damages, and lost productivity.

But a lack of sleep affects more than just our job performance. It affects the heart of our relationships.

Dr. Philip Collins of Fletcher Memorial Hospital reports that individuals who feel chronically tired have a lower tolerance for daily stress. They get bent out of shape more easily. They tend to experience poor interpersonal relationships as a result, and have more family break-ups.

A chronic lack of rest doesn't just affect our bodies. It affects our personalities; it affects our characters. Irritability can slowly become a habit. We stay bent out of shape more and more of the time. We think our wife is the enemy. We think our husband is the enemy. We think some co-worker is the enemy. And we get caught up in ugly incidents of "friendly fire."

Movie producer Jack Warner always took an afternoon nap in his office at Warner Brothers. And it was an unwritten rule that he should be left undisturbed. But one day, Bette Davis burst into the office while Warner was asleep and began ranting about a script she didn't like.

Without opening his eyes, Warner reached for the phone and called his secretary. "Come in and wake me up," he said, "I'm having a nightmare."

Warner resolved his little nightmare with a bit of humor. But for too many of us it's our chronic fatigue that produces more and more nightmares, more and more conflicts in waking life.

This is the irony so many of us are caught up in. In order to pursue what we think is a better quality of life, we cram too much into our days. We take less and less time to rest. As a result, our fatigue dramatically decreases the quality of our lives.

We're chasing after things we believe matter most. But then we can't enjoy them because of poor health. We're too tired to enjoy what we've worked so hard for.

We want to zero in on priorities. What should we concentrate on? What should we invest in? What will be of most value in the end?

In the last chapter, we focused on the spiritual dimension of our lives. That has to be a priority. Without a healthy relationship with God, very little that we pursue will be worthwhile.

Now we're looking at the physical dimension. What can we do to ensure the physical quality of our life? As I look around at our overburdened, frantic-paced lifestyles, one thing stands out—rest. The quality of our rest has suffered greatly.

Remember that it's not just the quantity of our rest that's important. It's the quality of our rest that counts— how deeply we rest, how well we're refreshed.

God is concerned about the quality of our physical lives. Many of us have terribly busy schedules, but I don't think anyone can claim to be busier than Jesus was. He had a very short time in which to accomplish His mission on earth.

While evading the plots of His enemies, Jesus had to change the course of history, found a church that would endure through the ages, and train His disciples to spread the gospel to the whole world. And through it all, He was healing the afflicted—night and day.

But look at what Christ Himself said in Mark. The apostles had just come back from a preaching tour and Jesus instructed them about quality living. He instructed them about life in its full abundance and He said: "Come aside by yourselves to a deserted place and rest a while. For there were many coming and going, and they did not even have time to eat" (Mark 6:31, NKJV).

Come aside and rest. Jesus was an incredibly busy man. But He cared about rest. He cared about His disciples resting. And God cares about the quality of our rest.

Listen to these verses from Isaiah: "In returning and rest you shall be saved; in quietness and confidence shall be your strength" (Isaiah 30:15, NKJV).

There you have it. And now, again from Isaiah, notice these words: "But those who wait on the Lord shall renew their strength; they shall mount up with wings like eagles, they shall run and not be weary, they shall walk and not faint" (Isaiah 40:31, NKJV).

Since we are wired for God, as we read in the last chapter, our hearts find rest in Him. The busyness of our lives often crowds Him out. It's not merely that our lives are crowded with bad things, it is that we often miss the things that matter most. And the one thing that matters most is knowing Him!

Sleep researchers tell us that one of the major culprits is late night television. If you want a good night's sleep, turn off the TV at least 30 minutes before you go to bed. If your mind is caught up in some emotional drama, you'll still be rehearsing those stories in your subconscious long after you try to go to sleep.

Too much TV interferes with the quality of our rest.

So does busyness, overwork. You'd think that you might sleep like a log after a hard day's work. That may be true after physical labor. But mental strain produces a restless night. We can't just shut off the stress at bedtime. It keeps us awake.

You may think that you HAVE to stay busy just to get everything done. But remember that in the long run, the quality of your life is going to suffer, the quality of your health is going to suffer.

Another thing to avoid is stimulants. Our bodies simply weren't made to function on caffeine, for example. Beware of drinks that have caffeine in them. They may be keeping you awake at night.

Also, avoid large meals late at night. You can't digest a lot of food and experience deep sleep at the same time. Something has to give. And since digestion won't wait, it's your rest that suffers.

But we can do more than just avoid the bad. We can also do positive things to improve the quality of our rest.

First, exercise regularly. At least 20 minutes of steady exercise three days a week is best. Walking is great! My wife and I often go out for a good, vigorous walk before bedtime. This alone can do wonders for your sleep. And it's a vital part of health in general. Recent research indicates that even a moderate amount of regular exercise significantly improves our long-term health.

And exercise in the open air. Get plenty of God's good fresh air into your lungs, and from there into your whole body.

Drink plenty of water. This is another one of those natural, miracle substances that we take for granted. Dehydration can lead to sleeplessness. Now I don't mean ten glasses right before you go to sleep, because you'll get plenty of exercise during the night if you do that. But be sure to take in at least seven or eight glasses of water spaced out through the day.

Finally, try to go to sleep at the same time each evening. Your body works best on a regular schedule, and it rests better, too, on a schedule that is consistent each evening. Deep rest is a matter of habit as much as anything else.

The average person needs seven to eight hours of sleep each night for optimal performance. Here's a good way to tell if you're getting enough. Can you get up in the morning without an alarm?

If you have to drag yourself out of slumber to punch the snooze button, your body is trying to tell you something.

Also, you should be able to go through the day without feeling a strong urge to lie down and sleep. Those feelings are your body's way of trying to get your attention. So listen up.

There are a few things you can do to sleep better. But we haven't touched yet on the most important factor, on the most important step you can take. For some people, what makes the difference between sleeping poorly and sleeping well is simply peace of mind.

Our emotional and mental state largely determines the quality of our rest. In the book of Ecclesiastes, we have a classic description of an individual without peace of mind: "For what has man for all his labor, and for the striving of his heart with which he has toiled under the sun? For all his days are sorrowful, and his work grievous; even in the night his heart takes no rest. This also is vanity" (Ecclesiastes 2:22, 23, NKJV).

If you find yourself wide awake in the dead of night, it may be because your heart is not at rest. You work hard, you accomplish a lot, but you're not sure what it all adds up to. You don't have peace.

Or there may be a moral problem, some hidden sin that's keeping you up. Nothing destroys peace of mind as thoroughly as a sin that we're trying to hide.

The book of Deuteronomy gives us a picture of what happens to people who are not honest with God, people who try to ignore His still, small voice. "In the morning you shall say, 'Oh, that it were evening!' And at evening you shall say, 'Oh, that it were morning!' because of the fear that terrifies your heart" (Deuteronomy 28:67, NKJV).

What a picture of restlessness! During the day you can't wait for night to come. And during the long, sleepless night, you can't wait for the morning. You always want to be somewhere else. Why? Because God isn't there with you. Because you've shut yourself off from Him in some way.

How do we find peace of mind once again? By opening up our fearful hearts to God, by taking that risk, by being honest with God about our mistakes. Peace of mind comes when God is present. Peace of mind comes when we open our hearts to God and find His peace.

In urging his people to trust in the Lord, the prophet Isaiah wrote these words: "You will keep him in perfect peace, whose mind is stayed on You . . ." (Isaiah 26:3, NKJV).

A mind fixed on God is a mind at peace. And we can have that peace of mind in any environment. Moses had one of the most stressful jobs on earth—leading a reluctant, unruly band of ex-slaves through the hostile desert to Canaan. They couldn't stop grumbling. But Moses stood like a rock of stability. God had given him a wonderful assurance.

This is what He told Moses in Exodus: "My Presence will go with you, and I will give you rest" (Exodus 33:14, NKJV).

God's presence is what gives us rest. It greatly improves the quality of our rest. Because He's the Good Shepherd. He's the One who can restore our souls, leading us beside the still waters and the green pastures.

Early on in his career, John Wesley found himself in the middle of a raging storm. He was sailing on the ship, *Simmons*, from England to America. Waves crashed into the boat and sent the passengers reeling into a state of panic. Even the seasoned crew thought they might go down into the deep.

Wesley was huddled below the decks with the others, trembling with terror. But he glanced over at one group of passengers and was shocked to observe them calmly singing a hymn. They were a group of devout Moravians whom Wesley had met earlier in the voyage and had spoken with. He'd sort of passed them off as heavy-minded and dull-witted folk.

But now, he stared in wonder. The more wildly the ship was tossed about, the more calmly these Moravians sang praises.

The storm finally subsided. And a deeply shaken Wesley just had to ask a question. He approached a young Moravian and inquired, "Were you not afraid?"

The man replied, "I thank God, no."

"But weren't your women and children afraid?" Wesley wondered.

"No," he answered, "our women and children are not afraid to die."

Wesley was trying to practice the Christian life at the time, but he realized these people had discovered a peace that was still foreign to him. He wanted to find out how they could proceed through a sail-ripping, skin-drenching storm without missing a beat.

The following day, Wesley struck up a conversation with a Moravian pastor named Spangenberg. He asked him the same questions.

After a while, the pastor said, "Does the spirit of God bear witness with your spirit that you are a child of God?"

Wesley was stumped. This was a new one. Spangenberg tried again: "Do you know Jesus Christ?"

Wesley replied, "I know He's the Saviour of the world."

"True, but do you know that He has saved you?"

Obviously, the Moravians had this knowledge, this still, small spot of assurance. They had come close to the eternal God and His peace enveloped them. It was a remarkable peace in the midst of a storm. Seeing that kind of peace moved Wesley to launch a more intense spiritual quest. Eventually, he would spearhead a great religious awakening in England.

The presence of God produces peace of mind.

Do you remember thunderstorms when you were a child? Do you remember how your mother might slip into the room? The thunder was raging, it was loud. The lightning was flashing. It was a very scary thing, wasn't it—especially when the storm came in the middle of the night.

But you'd call out, "Mommy," or "Daddy" and Mom or Dad would come running from their bedroom. And as soon as they sat down on your bed and took you in their arms, the thunder didn't seem so loud anymore; the storm didn't seem so big and scary anymore.

That's what the presence of God can do for us. His presence produces peace of mind.

There's a story that comes to us from the London bombings during World War II. German bombers pounded the city night after night. Whole neighborhoods turned into rubble, fires blazed everywhere.

It was an especially frightening time for children caught in a raid. And one little boy, peering out from a shelter, kept staring at the explosions in the distance. He stood there shaking and crying. But his father came quickly and turned his boy around and said firmly, "Face toward me. Face toward me."

During the rest of the night, when the bombs were screaming down, and the earth shook, the little boy would turn his face toward his father—and he'd stop shaking; the terror would drain from his face.

Our Heavenly Father is telling us, "Face toward Me." In your times of fear, "Face toward Me." In your times of anguish, "Face toward Me." When your life is out of control, "Face toward Me."

That's how we find peace of mind. The presence of God produces peace of mind.

Let's open our hearts right now to the One who created us, to the Father who knows us intimately, to the Father who loves us faithfully. God has gone to great lengths to bring us health and healing. He's gone to great lengths to bring us peace. Let's reach out to Him right now.

When Hugs Come Too Late

There's an awful lot of talk about family values these days—and how we need to return to the moral decency of a simpler, sunny era. Trying to clean up America is a worthy goal. But there are many people who feel sidelined from all of this. There are many people who would love to have family values. But their family failed to give that to them.

Can they ever find a place in the sun?

On Father's Day in 1995, Roy finally had his family around him. There were gifts, a big home-cooked meal, snapshots in the backyard, and lengthy visits with his grown daughter and son. He splashed in the pool with his baby grandchild. Everyone hugged when it was time to say goodbye.

Roy had always been a very public figure. In fact, he'd become a very famous champion of family values. And now, in that backyard scene, reality finally seemed to be measuring up to the rhetoric.

It hadn't always been that way.

Roy's son Mike keenly remembers the day of his graduation from high school. His dad had been asked to give the commencement speech. And afterwards he was shaking hands with a few of the graduates. Mike stood there

27

proudly in his cap and gown. His dad walked up and announced, "My name's Roy, what's yours?"

That's how Mike remembered the father who had disappeared from his life after his parents divorced. He grew up to write a bitter, tell-all book about his parents—people who seem to have had a hard time showing affection.

Then there was daughter, Penny. She ended up writing three books exposing her dysfunctional family. She described her mother, Roy's second wife, as a manipulative pill-popper. And she saw her father, Roy, as cold and remote.

Penny changed her last name to escape her famous Dad's shadow. She struggled with anorexia. She went through disastrous relationships. She posed nude in *Playboy* to flaunt her Dad's values.

Over the years, Mike and Penny had become completely alienated from their parents. They had absorbed very little nurture in their home.

But finally, on that Father's Day in 1995, the hugs did come. There was a sense of reconciliation as they posed for snapshots in the backyard.

Just one thing darkened the sunny scene. Roy, now in his 80s, was suffering from Alzheimer's. His memory had decayed. Family members had to shout into one ear to make themselves heard. Roy could talk and smile, but he wasn't always there.

On that Father's Day there were many embraces. But Roy didn't always know who he was hugging. His children finally had a dad generous with affection. But Roy couldn't always say their names.

Everyone knows that one of the things that matters most is family. Families shape us as human beings. There's nothing more important than the nurture that a father or mother can give. We need to do everything we can as a society to protect families and help them remain intact.

But what about the people whose families failed them? What about the many people who didn't grow up with loving parents? What do you do when the hugs come too late?

It's an important question. We're all deeply influenced by what happens in our childhood. We carry that around with us. It's baggage that we have to deal with. Many of us spend most of our lives reacting to what happened in our childhood. We don't all write bitter memoirs or pose for *Playboy*—but we react in some way.

And so one of the things that matters most in life is this: how do we deal with our past? How do we get over it? Do we remain handicapped by the bad things that happened? Do we keep looking for love in all the wrong places? Or do we find some other healthy source of nurture?

I'd like to suggest a different way in which you can get over the past and move on with your life.

I don't want to say this is an easy task that you can do in the next twenty minutes. A dysfunctional family affects our ability to receive love. We have a hard time absorbing the right kind of love later in life. We have a hard time giving it back.

Overcoming all this is a tremendous challenge. But right now I want to talk with you about an ally you may not have considered. I want to tell you about a source of nurture that you may even have ignored.

God's original plan is to nurture us through our families. That's what He designed life to be like. God reveals Himself through the love of a mother and father. God created the family as the perfect, secure environment where human beings could grow into healthy adulthood.

But did you know that God has a backup plan? Did you know that God has an alternative when things don't work out right?

Let me show you what that is. We first spot it in the Bible in Psalm 27. The psalmist is talking about his desire for intimate fellowship with God. And this is what he says in verse 10: "When my father and my mother forsake me, then the Lord will take care of me" (Psalm 27:10, NKJV).

What is this verse saying? When our family of origin fails us, who takes up the slack? God Himself. He offers to take care of us. He offers to parent us.

That's quite a promise. That's quite a backup plan!

Let's make sure we've got it right. Look at what Psalm 68:5 says: "A father of the fatherless, a defender of widows, is God in His holy habitation" (NKJV).

How does the Almighty identify Himself? As a Father of the fatherless.

Jesus Himself gives us the same assurance. Throughout His ministry He identified God as *our* Father in Heaven. He's the Father who knows how to give His children good gifts.

Unfortunately, people from dysfunctional families have a hard time receiving those gifts. Tragically, not getting love early on often prevents them from getting it later in life.

But look at this wonderful assurance from the apostle Paul: "For you did not receive the spirit of bondage again to fear, but you received the Spirit of adoption by whom we cry out, 'Abba, Father.' The spirit Himself bears witness with our spirit that we are children of God" (Romans 8:15, 16, NKJV).

Problems in our families often leave us in bondage to fear; insecurity follows us everywhere. But God steps in and offers to adopt us. And He does more. He offers us the "Spirit of Adoption." The Spirit can help us realize deep within that we are truly children of God. The spirit can move us to cry out, "Abba," "Daddy!"

The Spirit can help us absorb the unconditional love of a Heavenly Father. We desperately need that when we're struggling to overcome a dysfunctional past.

That is God's backup plan. Originally, He planned to reveal His love to us through loving families. But when that's not possible, he can reveal Himself directly—as our Heavenly Father, giving us the spirit of adoption.

Think for a moment about what that means.

Let's say you're a kid who'd like to learn to play basketball better. You're not much of an athlete. You're tired of being the last one chosen at pick-up games. So you plead with local players to teach you some good moves under the basket. Finally, a guy at the YMCA promises to coach you a little bit.

He says he'll meet you at the gym Sunday afternoon. And so you arrive with your Nikes on at one o'clock sharp. And you wait. But the guy never shows up—he's a flake.

You're really disappointed. However, just before you leave, a six-foot-nine-inch, slim, but muscular athlete walks onto the gym floor. He's wearing number 23.

The man runs up, dribbling a basketball and makes a flying leap from the free-throw line—for an amazing slam dunk. Then he turns to you and says, "Hi, sorry the YMCA guy didn't show. I'm Michael Jordan. Would it be OK if I coach you instead?"

Your mouth drops open. Would it be OK!? Yeah, I guess Michael Jordan—the man widely regarded as the best basketball player in all history—would work as the backup plan. He'd work as the alternative!

Friends, your parents may let you down, but the Heavenly Father promises to parent you, that's good news. It's a world-class Father who offers His nurture and integrity. He's got better gifts than anything an earthly father could come up with.

But there's even more to the divine backup plan. There's even more God does for us when hugs come too late.

Listen to God speaking through the prophet Isaiah.

"Can a woman forget her nursing child, and not have compassion on the son of her womb? Surely they may forget, yet I will not forget you. See, I have inscribed you on the palms of My hands" (Isaiah 49:15, 16, NKJV).

The inconceivable could happen. A woman could abandon her nursing infant. But God will never forget. He promises to write our name on His palms.

This text is telling us that God can give us Mother love. He's *our* Father in Heaven. But He also has all the tender mercy and compassion of a mother.

Did your mother let you down? Was she cold and distant? God has a backup plan. God promises to comfort us "As one whom his mother comforts" (Isaiah 66:13, NKJV).

Psalm 131 describes what trust in God can be like. Verse 2 gives us this picture: "Surely I have calmed and quieted my soul, like a weaned child with his mother; like a weaned child is my soul within me" (Psalm 131:2, NKJV).

A child in its mother's arms. What a picture! That's a picture God is giving us. He's saying, "That's what I can be for you."

But there's still more.

Ezekiel 16 gives us a graphic description of a baby girl who'd been abandoned out in an open field, loathed from the day she was born. But God comes by and sees her. And this is what He says: "I spread My wing over you . . . I swore an oath to you and entered into a covenant with you, and you became Mine . . . I clothed you with fine linen and covered you with silk . . . I put . . . a beautiful crown on your head" (Ezekiel 16:8, 10, 12, NKJV).

This is a picture of God as a passionate lover. He cherishes us as a bridegroom cherishes his bride. The prophets frequently describe God as longing for His unfaithful people like a jealous lover. Jesus gives Himself up for the church as a husband gives himself up for his wife.

Here's yet another part of God's backup plan. Have you

been rejected by a spouse? Do you feel abandoned, unwanted? God wants to choose you as His; He wants to cover you with silk and put a crown on your head.

God is more passionately devoted than any lover on earth.

All we need we have in Him.

In describing Jesus' ministry as a Man on earth, the author of Hebrews describes how the Saviour was made perfect through suffering. And then He says: "For both He who sanctifies and those who are being sanctified are all of one, for which reason He is not ashamed to call them brethren" (Hebrews 2:11, NKJV).

A little later we are told, "In all things He had to be made like His brethren" (Hebrews 2:17) Jesus took on our flesh and blood. He was tempted and tried in all the ways we are.

What does this mean? God has become our brother. He doesn't just have compassion as a parent. He suffered with us as a brother. He knows exactly what we're going through. He understands.

God is our Brother in Heaven.

Friends, when we understand these things about God, all we can say is What a family! There's a family in God! A complete family! We may have missed out on the faithfulness of a father. We may have missed out on the compassion of a mother. We may have missed out on the closeness of a spouse or brother or sister.

But there's a whole family *in* God. And He can reveal Himself directly. He can minister to us as father, as mother, as lover, as brother.

Dennis didn't just have a father who let him down. He grew up with a man who gave him a terribly distorted picture of what God is all about. Dennis' father bullied his children into submission. Instead of bedtime stories, he read the chapters in Deuteronomy that list curses on the disobedient.

Dennis grew into his teenage years embittered against this harsh authority figure. He rebelled against the fanatical religion of his father. And yet he mirrored him in many ways. He found himself arguing with everyone; he had a desperate need to be right all the time.

But then Dennis ran across something that woke him up. He read passages in the Psalms about the care of a Heavenly Father, some of the same verses we read earlier. And it began to dawn on him that maybe, just maybe, God was completely different from his own father. Maybe he'd really been trying to serve an endlessly demanding tyrant in the sky.

Dennis began reading the Scriptures with a different perspective. He discovered the gospel that Paul championed in his epistles. The fact that God could accept an individual completely—solely on the basis of what Christ did on the cross—seemed like an incredible revelation. God was gracious. A God like that could nurture.

Dennis began to understand and accept more and more of the gospel of grace. It took time. Old compulsive habits and attitudes didn't go away immediately. But in time, Dennis grew into something of a miracle.

He discovered in God the qualities of a caring father, an affectionate mother, a passionate lover, and an understanding friend.

He became the nurturing father of a boy and girl, two kids who I know love him dearly.

Dennis is the kind of dad whom kids love to cozy up to before they go to sleep.

He's the kind of dad who makes his daughter feel beautiful—because he tells her how special she is every day.

He's the kind of dad whom his son can look up to, because he leads by example.

Dennis didn't learn any of these things from his earthly father. Dennis didn't learn how to love from him.

Dennis became a wonderfully nurturing father because of God's backup plan. God became Dennis' parent. He nurtured this young man through His gospel of grace. And God was a good parent. God was a great parent. He reproduced His father-love in an individual who should have grown up stunted and bitter.

God's hugs didn't come too late. God's hugs came just in time.

Have you experienced the wonderful love of God the Father? Have you come to know that there's a family in God? There's a family there for you.

God can parent you in a special way if your biological parents let you down. You have a choice to make. You can go on carrying around all the baggage, trapped in the hurt and anger and insecurity. You can keep latching on to the negative. Or you can give that up to God the Father, God the Family. You can use the pain of your past to drive you deeper into His arms.

It may not be easy. But you can absorb God's unconditional love by investing yourself in a relationship with Him. Take a look at God the Father in the Bible. Look at how Jesus shows you what He's like. Meditate on the scenes of Christ's life. Meditate on psalms that picture God's nurture. Respond back to God in prayer, open up your heart to Him.

Make the investment. It's worth it. It's worth having God as a parent, believe me. He's the most wonderful parent in the world.

Getting off
the Mountain

They found Juanita at 20,000 feet in the Andes mountains—perfectly preserved in the ice. She was curled in a fetal position, wrapped in fine woolens of chocolate brown and cream-colored stripes. Juanita had soft brown hair and high cheekbones.

Why did this 13-year-old girl die on an isolated mountaintop, or had she been deliberately killed?

Answers to such questions help us to understand the mysteries of the gospel.

In the summer of 1995, Johan Rienhard set out on a reconnaissance trip in the wake of an erupting Peruvian volcano. It had been spewing hot ash on nearby ice-covered mountains.

Anthropologist Johan thought this might be a golden opportunity. He'd been exploring icy Andean summits for years in search of archeological remains of the great Inca civilization. Perhaps the volcano had dislodged something.

Finally, he reached the summit ridge of a mountain called Ampato. And he was stunned to find that the heat of the eruption had melted away the ice and snow. Johan spotted some feathers sticking out of the thin ridge. It proved to be the headdress of a small Inca statue.

And then something below the slope caught his eye. He

scrambled down and came upon the find of a lifetime—
the frozen, perfectly preserved body of an Inca girl. She
had tumbled from the summit as the snow melted around
her grave.

Johan examined the 500-year-old icy coffin of the girl
he would name "Juanita." He found shards of ceramic,
fragments of food, bits of wood, pieces of bone. She was
wrapped in fine woolens.

Johan believed he had come upon a ritual offering, a
human sacrifice. It appears that this child had been killed
by Inca priests to appease the gods, especially the god of
this volcanic mountain with its eruptions contaminating
the Incas' water supplies and destroying their crops 500
years ago.

As darkness fell, Johan took out a pick and began care-
fully separating Juanita from the ice that still encased
her. She had been locked in this frozen embrace, embed-
ded in the mountain by the ice, as a sacrifice, for five cen-
turies.

Juanita has given archeologists new insights into Inca
culture. Other mummies have been discovered on Andean
summits as well—all of them children without blemish,
all of them killed as sacrifices to the mountain god.

Johan believes that Juanita was brought to that summit ridge to be sacrificed, probably drugged to sleep and
buried alive. Something had to be done to appease the
angry mountain and quell the fire in its belly.

It's very hard for us today to imagine sacrificing a 13-
year-old girl to a mountain. We think we know better than
to try to appease a volcano.

And yet little Juanita, frozen in that icy summit for
half a millennium, pictures a dilemma we all face, a
struggle that involves us all, whether we realize it or not.

We struggle with guilt, a constant sense of condemnation. We stumble through life constantly wondering if we

are accepted or rejected by God.

Multitudes never think about God, yet they still possess a sense of emptiness. Even a beautiful, smiling face can portray an emptiness on the inside.

We wonder about God. Life can make us wonder whether we're under His curse or under His blessing.

Sometimes we nod our heads when people tell us how much the Father in Heaven loves us. At other times, we feel very far away from an absolute, holy God. In fact, the closer we come to the awesome Almighty, the more insecure we feel about our own standing.

People may not sacrifice children today to get closer to God. But we do all kinds of other things to make ourselves worthy for God to accept us. We have our rituals. We have our performance compulsions. We try in countless ways to be accepted.

And sometimes it all seems like a great mountain we're trying to climb. The more we try to be like God, or like Jesus, the more slippery the slope becomes, the more we realize how weak and selfish we are.

These attempts to make ourselves acceptable to God are called by theologians righteousness, or salvation, by works.

Attempting to be saved by our own works or our human efforts has plagued the human race since Adam and Eve fell into sin in Eden's garden.

When Adam and Eve sinned, they initially experienced a sense of exhilaration—a euphoric feeling that they were entering into a higher state of existence. But then suddenly a sense of terror and guilt filled their souls. The peace and joy that once filled their lives was replaced by anxiety and fear.

Their original joy was gone. Would it ever return? Would they ever have the place they once knew? Would they ever feel secure in God's presence again?

Adam and Eve decided that they must do something! They had to act. They fashioned makeshift garments to cover their nakedness. This was an attempt to achieve righteousness by works. They attempted to atone for their sin through their own actions.

Humankind ever since then has tried to atone for their sins by their works—by their own endeavors.

Satan is delighted to see the human race wallow in the mire of trying to do something—to have a sense of closeness to God. To feel accepted by Him.

The good news of the gospel is that God Himself decided to solve this fundamental human problem. In his letter to the Ephesians, the apostle Paul refers to the alienation that much of the world feels. He talks about people "without hope and without God in the world."

Then he makes this statement: "But now in Christ Jesus you who once were far off have been made near by the blood of Christ" (Ephesians 2:13, NKJV).

The blood of Christ brings us near to God. It is Christ's blood that reconciles us to God. His precious blood covers our sins.

But why did Jesus have to shed His blood and die in order to save us?

After all, if God really loves us, why can't He just forgive us, period?

Is God like some pagan deity who requires the human sacrifice of His Son? Is He like the so-called volcano god of the Andes requiring the sacrifice of His children?

That's a very important question. It's important because the Cross is at the very center of the Christian faith. And I believe, if we really understood the Cross, we wouldn't get caught up in a lot of the ritual that fills up so many religious lives. We wouldn't get caught up in a lot of religious actions that we hope will pay for our sins. We wouldn't have to keep climbing that huge mountain in order to be accepted by God.

In short, I believe the Cross is how we get Juanita off the mountaintop. We can end all the unnecessary sacrifices, these human efforts to appease, to be accepted, if we grasp what really happened at the cross.

Now, let's try to answer the question, "Why did Jesus have to die?"

We find the best step-by-step explanation in the book of Romans. Paul sets out in that epistle to present the doctrine of "justification by faith"—which is synonymous with the terms "righteousness by faith" and "salvation by faith" alone in Jesus Christ.

This is how sinful human beings can be accepted by a holy God.

Our alienation from God isn't just a feeling; it isn't something that we simply need to cope with or adjust to. It's based on one hard fact: "For all have sinned and fall short of the glory of God" (Romans 3:23, NKJV).

Sin separates us from God—this is a reality. When Adam and Eve fell into sin, their righteous, perfect natures were changed. Sin became a part of them. They now possess what we call a "fallen, sinful human nature."

The results of this placed all humanity under the penalty of death. Eve herself repeated God's words to the serpent who tempted her. Referring to the forbidden fruit, she exclaimed: "God has said, 'You shall not eat it, nor shall you touch it, lest you die.' " (Genesis 3:3, NKJV).

The apostle Paul explains this point clearly in Romans: "Through one man sin entered the world, and death through sin, and thus death spread to all men, because all sinned" (Romans 5:12, NKJV).

Now we come to the question, again, "Why did Jesus have to shed His blood and die to save us?" Why couldn't God just say, "I forgive you"?

One important aspect of the answer is simply this—

God is just. If God in His love would have overlooked our sin, Satan would have accused Him of being a liar. I can hear him say, "God, you said if Adam and Eve ate the forbidden fruit they would die. Now, you have changed your mind and instead of killing them you are forgiving them. You are not true to your word."

But that is not all! Had God destroyed Adam and Eve with no substitute plan to satisfy His justice—Satan and the universe would accuse Him of being a God of hideous wrath, hate, anger—an unjust, unloving God!

The results of this would be that the entire universe would serve Him through fear. God faced a very definite dilemma. Satan thought he had God on the defensive—in a corner!

But what did God do? He, along with Christ and the Holy Spirit, made a decision that literally astounded the universe and shocked Satan and his cohorts beyond description.

John 3:16 was God's answer to the fallen race. God's deliverance was solved. "For God so loved the world that He gave His only begotten Son, that whoever believes in Him should not perish but have everlasting life" (John 3:16, NKJV).

The inhabitants of the universe never dreamed that God would take such steps to redeem humanity. They never dreamed Jesus would reduce Himself to a microscopic cell or gene to be implanted in Mary's womb and be born in a barn in Bethlehem. Imagine the Son of God becoming the Son of Man. What love!

Furthermore, the death of Jesus for you and me on the cross forever shuts Satan's mouth. He could never call God a liar or accuse Him of being unjust or unfair.

Justice and mercy met together at the Cross. Jesus has forever identified Himself with the human race! This fact makes true Christianity the only religion on earth that is built upon love and not fear.

We serve Him, not because we fear Him but because He loves us with an everlasting love!

True, "the wages of sin is death." The entire human family deserves to die, but praise God our debt has been paid by the gold of Christ's blood and the silver of His tears. We are now saved from death if we accept His infinite sacrifice.

I ask you this question—what more could God have done to redeem us?

No wonder Paul asked the question: "Who shall separate us from the love of Christ? . . . For I am persuaded that neither death nor life, nor angels nor principalities nor powers, nor things present nor things to come, nor height nor depth, nor any other created thing, shall be able to separate us from the love of God which is in Christ Jesus our Lord" (Romans 8:35, 38, 39, NKJV).

Jesus became our substitute on the cross. He stands in our place. He gets what we deserve so we can get what He deserves. Paul puts it very clearly in 2 Corinthians: "For He [God] made Him [Christ] who knew no sin to be sin for us, that we might become the righteousness of God in Him" (2 Corinthians 5:21, NKJV).

God's salvation is a free gift. It is righteousness or salvation by faith, not by works. There's nothing we can do to earn salvation, to merit salvation, to buy salvation—it is God's gift of love to every human being who will accept it.

Justification by faith alone in Christ is lost sight of when one begins to invent ways and means of recommending himself or herself to God, of getting to heaven by his or her own merits.

Deep within the human heart, there is a desire to be one with our Maker. We may mask that desire, deny the inner conviction or quench the flame, but it is still there.

In our still, quiet moments, when we turn off the TV and the music stops, the inner voice of the Spirit draws us to God.

Unfortunately, this inner desire may lead us to manufacture ways to please Him—to attempt to earn His love.

A friend of mine, Harry, did just that! I watched his frustrated efforts to please God. He fasted, then wondered whether he should have fasted just another day longer. He prayed, then felt guilty for not praying another hour longer. He became paranoid about leaving his house! If he did, he might see an attractive woman and experience lustful thoughts.

Measuring himself with the ideal of Christ, he continually fell short. He certainly wasn't as patient, as compassionate, as kind as Jesus.

He condemned himself! No matter how hard he tried, Harry was a failure, a loser—condemned to eternal loss.

Then one day, in his regimented Bible study, he read: "For by grace you have been saved through faith, and that not of yourselves; it is the gift of God, not of works, lest anyone should boast" (Ephesians 2:8, 9, NKJV).

He read the passage again! And again! Could it be true? Did God love him that much?

Like the sun chasing away the darkness, a completely new thought struck him.

Salvation was based on Christ's works—not his.

Salvation was rooted in believing—not achieving.

Salvation was based on an act Christ had already done—not works he was trying to perform.

A new peace flooded into his life. A new joy radiated his entire being.

Friend, you can experience Harry's joy right now. Why not come to Jesus just as you are? Why not come with your faults, your sins, and all the rebellion in your heart?

He says: "The one who comes to Me I will by no means

cast out" (John 6:37, NKJV).

He will not cast you out, friend! Come, not with your own works to present but your goodness as a letter of recommendation to God.

Come believing.

Come in faith.

Come trusting in His righteousness.

Come resting in His love.

Come accepting His grace.

But come and come now!

I appeal to you to stop trying to be saved. Stop trying to make some sacrifice or some work to make you worthy. Stop trying to build security on the things you do. Please stop trying to make God accept you.

Simply come empty-handed to the sacrifice Jesus made on the cross. Yes, this is how much sin costs. Yes, this is how much God loves you. You have to come on His terms. He's laid them out very clearly—because that's the only way you can build a healthy, secure relationship with God.

Accept the life of Christ spilling out from the Cross. He offers it up for you. Accept His forgiveness. It's a marvelous forgiveness—not because of anything you do but because of how much He's done. Trust in Him as your substitute. You can be accepted by a holy God *in* the beloved Son. When He sees you, He sees Jesus.

Come to the Cross with nothing. No pretenses. No excuses. No credit. Nothing. Come because God has everything. Come because God wants to build you up from the ground level. He wants to recreate you.

Come into the drama of the Cross.

Coming to Be
With Me

What is it about certain people that makes their presence so—magical? Everybody wants to get near them; everybody wants to touch them; everybody wants to find out intimate details about their daily existence.

What kind of hold do celebrities fill in our lives?

Every morning when Frank wakes, Marilyn Monroe smiles down upon him—from a poster on the ceiling. It's a vintage movie poster, just one of his prized possessions. When he walks into his closet, he selects a pair of trousers just like the ones Warren Beatty wore in *An Affair to Remember*.

When he puts on his cologne, he can glance around at Michelle Pfeiffer, Sandra Bullock, and Brad Pitt—all in autographed photographs propped on his dresser, all sent from their respective fan clubs.

Frank grabs his camera bag and takes off across town to a nice little bistro in the Westwood section of Los Angeles. Rumor has it that Kiefer Sutherland may show up there with his new girlfriend. Frank wants to be ready to snap the couple as they hurry out of their limo. Certain magazines will pay good money for an exclusive shot.

Frank chases celebrities. That's his life. He's a paparazzi, trying to make a living from candid photographs of hard-to-capture movie stars.

And there's only one reason he can do that. Millions of people want to look at those photographs. Millions of people want to buy the magazines and newspapers that feature them.

Celebrities aren't just famous people. They're famous people with magnetic personalities. Sometimes those personalities may be imaginary—something that's projected from a movie screen. But they still have a powerful chemistry. People are drawn to them. People want into their lives. People want to be where they are. They fill some kind of hole in our lives.

Most of us lead pretty uneventful, unglamorous lives. Most of us lead pretty anonymous lives. But celebrities are somebody, somewhere.

And people who feel very unloved sometimes try to imagine that they have some kind of relationship with a celebrity. They have big holes inside them and believe that this magical person can fill those holes.

So they dress up like Captain Kirk of Star Trek.

Or they keep pouring their hearts out in letters to John Travolta.

Or they try to believe that Elvis is still alive—somewhere.

But of course most of us will never have a real relationship with a celebrity. It's not going to happen. They definitely don't want us to be where they are. They have to go to a lot of trouble to keep their privacy—bodyguards and high fences and disguises.

They have to lead very separate lives.

So, when we feel unloved, when we feel like nobodies, celebrities can't really help. Their presence may indeed be magical. They may indeed have magnetic personalities. But most of us can't have a real relationship with a celebrity. They remain just posters on the wall.

But there is one exception, one very remarkable exception.

I want to tell you about one celebrity who is very different. This is a world-famous, charismatic figure with a large following. His remarkable life has been portrayed in countless books and movies. People are quoting Him all the time.

Talk about the power to touch people. This celebrity could touch a leper and cure him. This celebrity's touch was enough to awaken the dead.

Talk about the power to move people. This celebrity held huge crowds captive to His every word.

He was the most charismatic personality in history. Everyone wanted to get close to Him. Everyone wanted to touch Him. Sometimes He had to withdraw from the public for awhile because the crowds became unmanageable.

But this celebrity is more than a poster on the wall. He doesn't just send back a newsletter when you pour your heart out. Listen to this celebrity's words in John: "In My Father's house are many mansions; if it were not so, I would have told you. I go to prepare a place for you. And if I go and prepare a place for you, I will come again and receive you to Myself; that where I am, there you may be also" (John 14:2, 3, NKJV).

This is Jesus Christ talking to His followers. He's about to return to His Father in heaven. He's about to return to His home, a place of unimaginable glory, a place ordinary human beings can only dream of visiting.

Christ deserves a place up there. He's the Beloved Son. His life on earth has been one of flawless love. He belongs in heaven with all its beauty and splendor.

But then Christ turns to His followers. He's talking to people with the usual human frailties. He's talking to men who get jealous and angry, men who think they're strong but who buckle in times of crisis, men who have a hard time "getting" spiritual things.

And Jesus says, "I'm going to prepare a place for you there." That's a place for *us*, a place for every single human who believes in Him, a place in heaven.

Why? Because Jesus wants us to be where He is. "Where I am, there you may be also."

The greatest celebrity of all time wants us in His neighborhood; He wants us living next door.

It's amazing that God gave up His Son for us. It's amazing that God became a man in order to rescue us from the plague of sin. It's amazing that Christ died on the cross in order to offer us pardon and acceptance with God. It's amazing that He rose from the dead to give us new life.

But perhaps the most amazing thing of all is this: Jesus wants us where He is—for all eternity! This isn't just a temporary housing arrangement. This isn't just a nice, polite, five-minute audience before the greatest celebrity of all time. This is eternal life with Jesus Christ. This is the thing that matters most.

You know, people who struggle with insecurity, people who feel like nobodies, try in all kinds of ways to build up their self-esteem. Their friends try to help in all kinds of ways.

And, let's face it, we all need affirmation. We all need to feel that we're somebody, that our lives count for something, that we're worth loving. So it's important to give and receive encouraging words.

But, did you know this? The second coming of Jesus Christ is the most encouraging word ever spoken. It overwhelms everything else. This should have an enormous impact on our self-esteem.

Jesus hasn't left us behind on earth. He's preparing a place for us in heaven. He's coming back to take us there. He wants us to be where He is—for all eternity.

Maybe in your fantasies, you've thought about what it would be like to live next door to Rembrandt or Albert

Einstein or John F. Kennedy. Wouldn't it be nice to have a backyard chat with them.

Well friends, Jesus Christ is the most charismatic personality of all time. And He's coming back, so that "Where I am, there you may be also."

A few people have experienced for a short time what it's like to be in God's full presence. They've experienced something like a face-to-face encounter in their hearts. Psalm 16 expresses the joy they have found there: "In Your presence is fullness of joy; at Your right hand are pleasures forevermore" (Psalm 16:11, NKJV).

The second coming of Jesus Christ is about God's presence. It's about the glory of God's presence. It's about a face-to-face encounter. And that leads to fullness of joy. That leads to a profound security.

Let me show you another way that Jesus pictures His second coming. In the parable of the wise and foolish virgins, He expressed it with this announcement, found in Matthew: "Behold, the bridegroom is coming; go out to meet him!" (Matthew 25:6, NKJV).

What is this saying? Jesus is coming back to earth for you with all the enthusiasm of a bridegroom coming to meet His bride. He's eager. He's passionate. He wants to sweep you off your feet.

He's coming back to seal your relationship forever in a covenant, a covenant as bonding and lasting as what He intended marriage to be.

The book of Revelation shows us what happens at the climax of the Second Coming. When Jesus does finally take us back to heaven, back to the place He has prepared for us—do you know what's first on the agenda? Revelation calls it "the marriage supper of the Lamb."

We're going to sit down to a great banquet. It's a marriage supper. The Lamb is Jesus Christ. We're going to be united with Him in a special way. We're going to celebrate the beginning of our eternal union with Him—next door.

And make no mistake. There may be millions of people in heaven. But Jesus is capable of making individuals feel that He is totally present just with them. He is a supernatural being. He's a supernatural celebrity, if you please. His abilities are infinite. That's why you can experience a face-to-face encounter, one-on-one. That's why He says, I've prepared a place JUST FOR YOU.

Friends, God's presence creates a wonderful security. Let me give you just one remarkable example.

Hedy became a fashion model at the age of 13—and jumped on the fast track to success. She got a contract with one of the top agencies in Chicago; she began appearing in TV commercials; she began winning beauty contests.

And this lovely young woman had brains too. She'd done well in some very good schools. She was artistically gifted and showed real talent as a painter.

Hedy had just about everything—except intimacy. She had plenty of dates. There were always men seeking her company. But she could never open up. She was always afraid that if people saw what was inside her, they would find her unlovable.

What Hedy had inside her was a big hole. It was a big empty space which a father's love should have filled. But Hedy's Dad was the kind of man who didn't express affection very well. He couldn't show tender feelings. He could never say the words that his daughter was secretly dying to hear: "You're special; I love you."

So, Hedy naturally struggled to win acceptance from everyone around her. She was always trying hard to win friends in school. She was always working to impress people.

She thought becoming a fashion model might help. She thought winning beauty contests might help. She thought appearing on TV might help.

It didn't. Nothing filled up that hole.

So what did Hedy do? She just kept trying. She moved to Hollywood and tried to start a new career in movies. Her pretty face got her on some nighttime talk shows. And she began networking with the right people. Soon she'd landed a few minor parts in feature films.

But the hole was still there. Hedy hung out with all the right celebrities at exclusive parties. She rubbed shoulders with some of Hollywood's biggest stars. She had a lot of "relationships." But they all fell apart very quickly. She still couldn't let anyone look inside. The hole was just too big.

Finally, Hedy moved back to Chicago. Still trying. Still hoping. She became a successful socialite, very active in civic affairs. She moved in society's upper crust. More celebrities. More relationships. But nothing filled that hole. That pressure to try to make people like her just never let up.

Finally, completely worn down by the process, Hedy and a boyfriend attempted a double suicide. They drove a car into a stone wall.

Hedy survived. And while recuperating from her injuries in a hospital, a nurse told her about a very different kind of celebrity, Jesus Christ.

Hedy started getting to know more about Him. Here was a Man who saw into the hearts of everyone around Him, and yet He loved people so unconditionally. Remarkable.

Hedy decided to give her life to this Man, this Saviour. And she discovered something about Him. She discovered that He could be present, really present, in a way that no other celebrity, no other personality, could.

In her own words, this is how she describes her encounter: "I kept saying over and over to myself, 'I can't believe it, Lord, I can't believe it.' What I had been demanding and waiting for from my father was the unconditional love of God, the Father. And now I could feel that love. A loving Father's presence seemed to be in the room with me, telling me silently, 'It's all right Hedy, you don't have to work; you don't have to be a star . . . to win my love and acceptance. You already have it—all you ever want. I'm your Father, Hedy, and—you're home, at last.' "

Lying there in that hospital ward, Hedy could hardly speak because of her extensive injuries. But, in what she called her bullfrog voice, she wanted to tell the whole world, "This is it. This is what everyone is looking for."

What can fill up the hole in people's lives? The presence of God. God being truly with us.

We can try all kinds of other things. We can spend our whole lives trying to stuff other things into that hole. But they just wither away. We haven't found the thing that matters most.

Friends, the second coming of Christ is about Jesus being present with you. It's the ultimate assurance that we need. "I'm coming back. I want you to be where I am." That's security.

And please remember, this is going to be a very real, physical reunion. The Second Coming is not some mystical event. It's not just something that takes place in the hearts of the pious. It's not just something we imagine.

Paul tell us very plainly in 1 Thessalonians: "For the Lord Himself will descend from heaven with a shout, with the voice of an archangel, and with the trumpet of God. And the dead in Christ will rise first. Then we who are alive and remain shall be caught up together with them in the clouds to meet the Lord in the air. And thus we shall always be with the Lord" (1 Thessalonians 4:16, 17, NKJV).

Thus we shall always be with the Lord. What powerful

words. We're really going to heaven with Him. We're not just going somewhere in our heads. We'll be caught up in the clouds to begin our journey with Him to the place He's prepared for us.

Revelation gives us this vivid picture: "Behold, He is coming with clouds, and every eye will see Him . . ." (Revelation 1:7, NKJV).

Every eye will see Him. Your eye will see Him. What emotions will go through you at that moment?

Is this the One you've been waiting for? Is this the One you've established a relationship with?

That's the real difference between human celebrities and Jesus Christ. We can't have a real relationship with a celebrity. We don't live in their world. They will never come off those posters on the wall. It's impossible for them to really care about all their fans. They can't transform nobodies into somebodies.

But Jesus is very different. We *can* have a real relationship with Him—starting right now. We can experience His presence in our hearts right now. He can nurture. He can love. He can fill that hole in our hearts.

How do we know? Because He's coming again.

How can we be sure? Because He's coming again. He promised.

Do you want to be ready for Jesus' return? Do you want Him to prepare a place for you in His Father's house? Do you want to look forward to that face-to-face encounter?

Then start a real, honest relationship with Him right now. Let Him look inside. Let Him see everything. Lay it all at His feet.

Your Law Is Too Small

Nice kids from nice homes in nice neighborhoods.

The kind of kids who do well in school and have clear goals for their future.

How then could they possibly be connected to a baby in a dumpster and a young girl lying in a field with two bullets in her head?

David was a handsome, clean-cut athlete with apparently high ideals. He'd fallen in love with a cute, dark-eyed honor student named Diane. Both attended high school in a pleasant, middle-class suburb of Fort Worth, Texas.

These model youngsters managed to earn highly competitive appointments to service academies in 1996. They were profiled in Fort Worth papers.

But then, Diane told two roommates at the Annapolis Naval Academy that she and her boyfriend shared a secret they would "take to their graves." Diane and David were soon linked to the gruesome murder of a 16-year-old classmate, Adrianne Jones.

David made a statement to police after his arrest. He and Adrianne were both on the track team. When he was driving her back from a meet one day, she'd seduced him. David confessed to Diane. His girlfriend was outraged by the betrayal.

David's statement read: "When this precious relationship we had was damaged by my thoughtless actions, the only thing that could satisfy her womanly vengeance was the life of the one that had, for an instant, taken her place."

So David made a date with Adrianne and drove her to a deserted place with Diane allegedly hiding in the back of the car. According to David, Diane struck her rival with a set of weights. Adrianne managed to run off into a field. David tracked her down and put two bullets in her head.

Afterward the couple vowed their undying love to each other, cleaned up their clothes, and drove to their homes.

Adrianne's murder raised troubling questions in 1996. How could youthful ideals be twisted into such an act of cruelty? How could nice kids, some of the best kids in our midst, be doing such things?

But the year wasn't over.

In December, we heard about Amy and Brian.

Both kids came from well-to-do, stable homes. Both were described by friends as "good kids." Both attended high school in a New Jersey suburb of golf courses and million-dollar homes. Amy excelled in her art classes. Brian was captain of the golf team and co-captain of the soccer squad.

They seemed an ideal match. Then Amy got pregnant and both kids apparently decided to hide the fact from their parents. They went away to different colleges, but still visited each other frequently.

Late one night, Amy called Brian, saying she thought she might be in labor. He drove three hours to her dorm and took her to a nearby Comfort Inn. What happened next pushes the story into dark tragedy.

Police say that a healthy boy was born toward morning. Brian told authorities that he placed the infant in a plastic bag and left him in the hotel dumpster.

But when police found the baby, they observed that its skull was crushed. Amy and Brian were indicted for murder.

More questions about the "best kids" in our midst. What could compel them to do such a thing to a newborn? What were they so afraid of? What were they so determined to avoid?

Friends, something is happening in our world today. More and more we're confronted with lawlessness in unexpected places. Newspaper headlines and tabloid news shows have accustomed us to gruesome crimes. But now we're seeing the inexplicably cruel where we least expect it.

If "good kids" can do this, we wonder, what can we expect from the children of abuse and deprivation? If kids with a bright future before them can take such devastating detours—what hope is there for everyone else?

No one, of course, can see into the minds of Amy and Brian. No one can really know what happened in the hearts of David and Diane. Every individual has their own story, their own moments of truth.

But I would like to suggest that tragedies like this should serve as a wake-up call. They are shocking, but the shock needs to teach us something. We need to wake up, because we've been in a moral slumber for so long. We've been drifting off for so long.

That moral slumber has taken a long time to develop. We've sunk into it gradually, with a thousand little unconscious compromises. It has to do with the way that we see ourselves as human beings. And the way we look at God.

Take, for example, the slogan, "To err is human." This isn't an unhealthy perspective, at first. People do need to know they're not perfect; they commit sins. But slowly, this fact has been turned on its head: now people seem reassured that they're NORMAL by their sins; people have come to identify their humanity by their moral failures.

"I'm only human" commonly means "I make mistakes." Fine. But does that mean that pursuing moral integrity is somehow less human?

Lately, we've begun connecting maturity and adulthood with one thing: our capacity to sin seriously. Vice is an "adult" thing. "G" ratings are for kids. The author of *The Second Sin* wrote this recently, "A child becomes an adult when he realizes he has a right not only to be right but also to be wrong." A *New York Post* columnist writes: "The greatest right in the world is the right to be wrong." These are the slogans of a secular age.

Of course, it's very important to acknowledge that we all struggle with moral problems. The tragedy is when people give up the struggle to obey a moral authority outside themselves, higher than themselves. What's at issue, and what has changed, is our goal as human beings, our identity, what we perceive as the good life.

In the Bible, we find a very different perspective on what human beings really are. We find a very different way to know ourselves.

Look at this picture from the book of James. In this passage, he's talking about the Word of God, and how we get our bearings from it: "For if anyone is a hearer of the word and not a doer, he is like a man observing his natural face in a mirror; for he observes himself, goes away, and immediately forgets what kind of man he was. But he who looks into the perfect law of liberty and continues in it, . . . this one will be blessed in what he does" (James 1:23-25, NKJV).

Notice what's being suggested here. The Word of God, the law of God, is like a mirror. When we look into it we can discover what kind of people we are. Some don't really pay close attention; they don't linger before that mirror long enough to make discoveries about themselves. Or else they run away from those discoveries. Others continue looking into that mirror; they respond to what it tells them about themselves—and they are blessed.

We don't really know who we are as human beings until we come face to face with the law of God. Why? Because God created us as moral beings. That's at our core. We have to respond to the moral voice of God, or we become something less than human.

Christ pictured this same basic truth through a parable. It's found in Matthew 7. He spoke of a wise man who built his house on solid rock and of a foolish man who built his house on shifting sand. When a storm came, the first house stood firm, the second was washed away.

And what lay behind one man's wisdom and the other's foolishness. Christ said the difference was this: one man listens to His teaching and takes it to heart; the other hears His teaching and ignores it.

In other words, when we build our lives on the teachings of Christ, we're building on solid rock. That's how healthy human lives develop. It's one of the things that matters most in life.

That's why God urges us to:

Pay careful attention to His Word (Hebrews 2:1).

Let it dwell in you richly (Colossians 3:16).

Take it to heart (Revelation 1:3).

Do what it says (James 1:22).

Live by every word (Matthew 4:4).

But for a long time now we've been inching out from under the law of God. We've lost a sense of how much our identity is tied in with God's moral voice.

We've been told over and over to just listen to the voice of our hearts; that's enough. We've been told over and over to find our own truth, our own identity—apart from God's moral purpose for our lives.

That perspective has been sinking in for a long time. And now we're beginning to see the results: lawlessness in unexpected places. Nice kids from nice families grow up with all of life's advantages—except this sense of obligation to God, this sense that they can't just make up the rules as they go along. They can't justify killing someone because it will make their lives so much easier.

There's something we need to remember about life on

the other side of God's moral voice, on the other side of His law, His principles. It's cruel over there. Friends, sin is cruel. It's hurting other people, or yourself. Take a good look, every time people fail morally, somebody suffers. And it's usually the weaker and more dependent who must suffer for the "humanity" of the stronger.

Sin is cruel. What if, instead of our familiar slogan, "To err is human," we started saying, "To be cruel is human. I'm only human, I've got to be cruel?" That doesn't sound so good, does it? But that's what is happening in our shrinking world.

A very famous American actor once met a lovely, fun-loving woman named Sharon. He fell in love with the girl. But there was a big problem. An admiring biographer put it this way: "He was a very married man who took his obligations seriously."

So did this man of virtue end the relationship right away? Not quite. The biographer tells us that he did not sleep with Sharon right away. The secret romance was restricted to a few kisses.

But then he walked into his wife's bedroom and told her that he'd met someone and wanted a divorce. She accepted this rather quietly and even wished her husband good luck. "She was absolutely wonderful," the actor recalled.

Well, her complete nervous breakdown wouldn't come until a little later.

The actor closed the door on his wife and went out to start a new life, greatly relieved that he'd done the right thing. These were his words, "I had been honest with my wife, fair to my children, virtuous toward Sharon, and finally, honorable with myself."

Astounding! How do we get to the point of seeing so much virtue in such an act. It's like complimenting someone on a nicely healing lobotomy—completely unaware of all that's been destroyed.

This is the kind of moral world we end up with when

obeying a higher moral authority is no longer important, no longer part of what makes us human. It's human to err. As long as we're polite in our cruelty and don't make a scene, we can walk away with our head held high.

It's tragic. Our moral horizons have been steadily shrinking for some time. We only talk about the law within our own hearts; we only ascribe to the rules we make up.

Well friends, that law is too small. It's just not big enough. It's just not compelling enough. It doesn't pull us up to higher ground. It just leaves us where we are.

Some time ago, J.B. Phillips wrote a book called *Your God Is Too Small*. He called people who'd been shrinking God down to their own size to take a good look at the awesome God of the Bible.

Well, after years of shrinking God into the size of our own hearts, we've reduced His moral voice to a whisper, one little voice among many others. And it's time for us to realize, "Your Law is too Small."

We live in a shrunken world today. This is the kind of moral world our kids have grown up in. Our law is just too small. That's why we're seeing lawlessness in unexpected places. That's why even the best among us are losing their way.

Against these shrinking horizons, the Bible presents something that can expand us, something that can open up our eye. Scripture looks at God's law in a special way. His commands aren't petty or burdensome. They give us insight; they are a delight.

The psalmists wax eloquent about the commands of God; they describe His precepts as trustworthy, radiant, pure, enduring forever, more precious than gold. (Psalm 19)

For the writers of Scripture, the law was larger than life in this sense—it encompassed all of life.

Here's a verse from Psalm 119: "Your word, O Lord, is eternal; it stands firm in the heavens" (Psalm 119:89, NIV).

Do you catch the picture here? The law, God's moral

voice, spreads out over us like the sky. It covers us—from horizon to horizon. It covers all of life.

Look at Psalm 36: "Your faithfulness reaches to the clouds, Your righteousness is like the great mountains; Your judgments are a great deep" (Psalm 36:5, 6, NKJV).

There is great breadth and depth and height in God's moral voice. God's law spread out like the heavens is God's wisdom spread out like the heavens. If we're to find a place for ourselves, if we're to find a place to stand, we need to make sure we're standing under God's law.

At the age of 33, Glenn Loury had become a tenured professor at Harvard. His career as an economist was skyrocketing. When Glenn spoke on public policy issues, people listened. But his personal life was crashing around him. He'd wandered into lawlessness—even in this most unexpected place: the campus of a great American university.

Glenn's use of alcohol and marijuana, on social occasions, had progressed into a cocaine habit. He'd become a regular user, and his wife couldn't get him to stop. He had the usual excuses, "Everybody's doing it." Glenn wasn't breaking his own rules. That seemed good enough.

But life outside God's law got worse and worse. Glenn progressed to free-basing his cocaine. He was killing himself. Arrested for possession, Glenn was ordered by a court into a treatment program. But he kept using.

Things got even worse. Sometimes, Glenn's wife could persuade him to go in for serious treatment, and he'd get clean. But then, after a few weeks, he'd relapse.

Finally, he moved to a half-way house run by an ex-cop, ex-alcoholic who'd become a Christian. Glenn began attending recovery meetings every night. And on Wednesday night he dropped in on the voluntary Bible study at the house.

During the next six months, Glenn absorbed the Word of God. A visiting pastor began counseling with him and got him into a second Bible study group.

Glenn was moved to make a commitment. It wasn't just to stay off drugs. It wasn't just to stay clean. He decided to stand under that broad sky, under the heavens of God's wisdom; God's moral voice became very real to him as he studied intently. He'd absorbed a very different perspective. "Everybody's doing it," wasn't good enough anymore.

Glenn committed his life to Christ. And he experienced profound changes in a life that had been out of control. This is how Glenn remembers it: "It just seems miraculous to me. It was miraculous that the desire to do cocaine went away. It was miraculous that my wife stayed by me and that the marriage came back to life again. It didn't have to happen. I haven't looked back."

Today, Dr. Glenn Loury continues to write and speak as a well-known economist. But now, his public life and his private life are in harmony, both are lived under the broad sky of God's moral voice. When he speaks about how spiritual issues affect economic issues, about what happens when God gets into the ghetto, Dr. Loury is speaking from the heart. He's speaking from experience. His law is big enough.

Have you found your place under that sky? Are you listening to God's moral voice? Or are you making up the rules as you go along? Is your law too small?

We need to find ourselves again—in that safe place under God's will. We desperately need the breadth of God's law in a time when lawlessness keeps appearing in unexpected places. We need that foundation in our lives. We need those boundaries.

Will you decide right now that you're going to help turn the tide, that you're going to stand in the right place? Once you've made a commitment to God, once you've established a relationship with Christ, as Glenn Loury did, God can begin fulfilling His law in your life. He can begin expanding you in the breadth of His eternal principles.

Let's make that commitment now.

The Surprise
of a Lifetime

She was the pride of the twenty-two-ship Townsend
Thoresen fleet, a magnificent vessel christened the *Herald of Free Enterprise*. The ship ferried passengers and
vehicles across the English Channel in first-class comfort.
At 433 feet and close to 8,000 tons, she could weather most
any storm.

And yet, on the night of March 6, 1987, its passengers
experienced a terrifying surprise. One hundred and ninety
men, women, and children were to lose their lives in a
matter of seconds. And how could it be, people wondered,
that such a tragedy occurred—just because someone forgot to close a door?

Everything was so routine about the ship's preparations
for the crossing from Belgium to England. The crew had
done it all countless times before. The *Herald of Free Enterprise* was a "ro-ro" a roll-on, roll-off ferry. Hundreds of
vehicles and passengers could come aboard very quickly
through massive steel bow doors.

At 7:05 PM on this gray winter's evening, the *Herald*
began backing out of her dock at Zeebrugge Harbor. The
sea was calm and the easterly wind light.

Loading officer Leslie stood at a control panel on G deck
where vehicles were parked. Across the dimly lit deck, he

spotted someone in orange overalls, weaving between cars toward the bow. He thought it was a crew member named Mark. It was Mark's job to close the 12-ton hydraulically operated bow doors. Satisfied that the job would get done, Leslie walked back up a stairway toward the bridge.

Mark, however, was in his quarters—fast asleep. Like the rest of the crew, he was working a 24-hour shift. After maintenance duties that afternoon, he decided to make himself some tea in his cabin. Feeling very tired, he sat on his bunk and opened a book. Mark fell asleep almost immediately. And he slept through the call to harbor stations.

The captain of the ship, Captain Lewry, might have noticed that the bow doors were still open. Bright, dockside lights were shining on them, and they were just visible below the bridge. But the ship was backing out of her berth, and the Captain was facing the stern. By the time the *Herald* swung around, she was in darkness.

At 7:20 PM the ship accelerated into the main shipping channel. A bow wave began piling up under her blunt prow. As the Herald picked up speed, churning white water broke over the top of the car deck. It started rushing in at the rate of 200 tons a minute. The open vehicle deck ran almost from one end of the ship to the other. There was nothing to interrupt the flow of the sea into the *Herald*.

At that moment passengers were stretching out comfortably in the lounges, chatting or dozing off. Many had filled the restaurants on board or lined up at the duty-free shop. Everyone was feeling quite warm and safe.

But at 7:27 PM, the vessel began rolling over on its port side. There was a moment's pause as crew and passengers wondered, What on earth is going on? Then the ship went over on its side and started to sink. The sea rushed in through windows in the upper decks. Those who weren't crushed to death or drowned tried to climb to safety. They found themselves clutching at lighting fixtures or ledges to work their way to what was now the top of the ship.

What happened suddenly one night on board the *Herald* was the worst British peacetime marine disaster since the sinking of the *Titanic*. It was so completely unexpected. In a matter of seconds, the world inside the *Herald* had turned upside down. One instant you were chewing on a deli sandwich, the next you were crashing through tables toward the port side. One instant you were paying for a souvenir, the next you were wrenched away by a rush of icy sea water.

How could anyone be prepared for that?

You know, the Bible speaks of another soon-coming event that will seem like a sudden disaster to many people. It tells us that the tragedies striking the world today are building up to the great climax of history. It's actually a glorious event, but that event will strike some people with all the terror of a thief breaking into your home at midnight.

Look at how the apostle Paul describes it in 1 Thessalonians: "For you yourselves know perfectly that the day of the Lord so comes as a thief in the night. For when they say, 'Peace and safety!' then sudden destruction comes upon them, as labor pains upon a pregnant woman. And they shall not escape" (1 Thessalonians 5:2, 3, NKJV)

What is this "day of the Lord"? It's the second coming of Jesus Christ. It's what Jesus promised to do before He left this earth. He said He would be preparing a place for His followers in heaven, and that He would come back again to take them home.

The Second Coming is a glorious event. But for some people it's like a thief in the night. While everyone's saying "peace and safety!" sudden destruction comes. It's as traumatic as labor pains.

But it doesn't have to be that way. Your world doesn't have to turn upside down when Jesus comes. It can, in fact, turn right side up. Look at the rest of this passage in 1 Thessalonians: "But you, brethren, are not in darkness, so that this Day should overtake you as a thief. You are all sons of light and sons of the day. We are not of the night nor of darkness. Therefore let us not sleep, as others do, but let us watch and be sober" (1 Thessalonians 5:4-6, NKJV).

People who've made a commitment to Jesus Christ, the Light of the World, are called children of light. They're not groping about in the dark anymore. They have a Friend who guides them toward a secure future.

And so, Paul says, if you belong to the day, don't fall asleep. Stay spiritually awake, in other words. Watch and be sober. Or, as other translations put it, "be alert and self-controlled."

When Jesus returns, He will appear like a thief in the night only to those who are sleeping. To those who are awake, He will appear as a wonderful Friend and Saviour.

So it matters a great deal whether we're asleep or awake at the second coming of Jesus Christ. That's an important event. Human destinies will be decided. It's one of the things that matters most in life.

So let's look at WHY people start falling asleep spiritually—especially as it relates to Christ's coming again.

First of all, we have to admit that it seems a long, long time since Jesus promised to come back. Two thousand years is a long time to be waiting. And so it's easy for people to just forget about it or push it into the distant future. It becomes less real. You focus on other worries, other hopes.

Interestingly enough, the Bible anticipated this state of mind. It anticipated what would happen when the coming of Christ seems delayed. Look at how the apostle Peter describes it in 2 Peter: "scoffers will come in the last days . . . saying , 'Where is the promise of His coming? For since the fathers fell asleep, all things continue as they were from the beginning of creation' " (2 Peter 3:3, 4, NKJV).

"All things continue." People look at the seasons come and go through the years. The pattern never changes. Generations come and go. Human life goes on. It's hard to imagine any big supernatural interruption.

And they have a point. Sometimes it *is* hard to imagine Jesus bursting through the heavens.

So what's Peter's answer to the scoffers? What assurance does he offer us?

He says that these skeptics are forgetting one important thing—that the Creator fashioned the heavens above us and made the earth to stand below us. That He once covered the world with a flood.

What's Peter's point? Well, he's getting at the real issue behind all the skepticism and doubt. The real issue is—Who's in charge? Who's ultimately controlling history? When things go on and on pretty much the same it's easy to assume that *we're* in charge. We unconsciously move God out of the picture. He's out there in some other dimension, we think, not really sovereign over this planet.

So Peter says, "Just stop and think about who made all this. God created this planet, and the whole universe, by His Word. It all came about at His command. The One who began it all is quite capable of ending it all. His Word is still powerful."

And Peter goes on to make this point in 2 Peter: "But the heavens and the earth which now exist are kept in store by the same word, reserved for fire until the day of judgment and perdition of ungodly men. But, beloved, do not forget this one thing, that with the Lord one day is as a thousand years, and a thousand years as one day. The Lord is not slack concerning His promise, as some count slackness, but is longsuffering toward us, not willing that any should perish but that all should come to repentance" (2 Peter 3:7-9, NKJV).

God is not just slacking off. It's not laziness that has delayed His coming. He's still very active in human life. And that activity centers around one thing: rescuing people, bringing people to repentance. He doesn't want to lose one single human being.

We may not understand the divine time table. We may not understand how things work from an eternal perspective where a thousand years is like one day. But we can know this—God is working to rescue human beings, and that rescue will climax in the second coming of Jesus Christ.

In Peter's mind, we can be as sure of that as we can be sure that there's a sky above us and an earth beneath us.

But people forget that. They forget about the Creator. They forget about the promise—it was made so long ago. And they start falling asleep spiritually.

How do you fall asleep spiritually? How does that happen? Well, first of all, you're lulled to sleep by routine. The daily grind, the weekly schedule—these things start capturing all our attention.

What happened aboard the *Herald of Free Enterprise* is instructive. Opening and closing that bow door was such routine. They'd done it scores of times. No one was alert; no one made absolutely sure the door was closed.

Routine lulls us to sleep. We get up, go to work, get back home, watch some TV, make a few calls, go to sleep. We get enough food in our bellies; we provide for our families. It's easy to forget about the spiritual dimension of our lives. We just let it slide. It becomes less and less real, less and less important.

Routine lulls us to sleep. Jesus identifies this very problem in Matthew: "For as in the days before the flood, they were eating and drinking, marrying and giving in marriage, until the day that Noah entered the ark, and did not know until the flood came and took them all away, so also will the coming of the Son of Man be" (Matthew 24:38, 39, NKJV).

There's nothing wrong with eating and drinking and marrying. They're good things. They're healthy things. But if that's all we're doing, then the flood, the end, will take us by surprise. Caught up in the pressure of little things, little duties, we forget about the big things, the big duties. We don't close the door, and the flood comes in.

On the *Herald* everyone assumed that someone else was taking care of it. Everyone was looking the other way. It was easy to fall asleep.

We make similar assumptions in the spiritual life. Someone else will take care of it. The church will take care of it. If my name is on the books, then that ought to take care of my spiritual needs. The pastor will take care of it. I sit through his sermons. I put in my time in the pew. That ought to take care of my spiritual needs.

Who's making absolutely sure that the door is closed? That's up to each individual. We have to take that responsibility. No one else's spirituality is going to count for us in the end.

When the frigid waters of the English Channel rushed into the *Herald* and that huge ship rolled over on its side, passengers were thrown in all directions.

A young couple, Susan and Rob, had just ordered dinner when it happened. They were sitting just a few feet apart at the table. Both clutched at furnishings as the ship rolled. Both were stunned when the water rushed over them.

But Susan tumbled underwater up to a passageway.

She managed to hang on to a shelf there—and was rescued.

Rob didn't make it. Susan would never see him again.

That's the way it went. Two people sitting side by side in the lounge—one would be thrown out a window by the water and up to safety. The other would be crushed in the debris. Two people walking on an upper deck—one would clutch a stairway and clamber to rescuers. The other would miss a handhold by inches and fall into the deep.

Destinies were decided in a few seconds. Something like that is going to happen at the second coming of Jesus Christ. Look at how Jesus describes it in Matthew: "That is how it will be at the coming of the Son of Man. Two men will be in the field; one will be taken and the other left. Two women will be grinding with a hand mill; one will be taken and the other left" (Matthew 24:39-41, NIV).

After making this statement, Jesus said, "Therefore keep watch." Why is one taken and the other left? Because one is sleeping and the other is awake. Both working in the field. Both grinding at the mill. Apparently doing exactly the same things. But one spiritually dead and the other spiritually alive. For one, Jesus comes like a thief in the night. For the other, Jesus comes as a long-awaited friend.

Yes, there are going to be some heart-wrenching dramas on that day. Suddenly the sky seems to split open. This brilliant cloud of light is falling toward the earth. No one has ever seen anything like it. Something like a trumpet sounds in the bursting sky—and that sound seems to circle the earth, and it pierces every heart.

Jesus is coming to earth like some exploding satellite, surrounded by what seems to be a galaxy of angels.

One secretary filing a budget report at her desk looks up—and is petrified. It's the surprise of a lifetime. In one instant she knows she's been sleeping all these years. She's been pushing God away. Another secretary at a desk right beside her looks up from her computer—and gasps in wonder. It's happened! It's really happened! In one instant, she knows that eternal life with her Friend, Jesus, is beginning—right now.

One will be taken up to heaven—and the other left behind on an earth soon to be destroyed.

One man at a gas station, filling his sedan with unleaded, looks up—and starts shaking uncontrollably. It's the surprise of a lifetime. Immediately he knows that everything he scoffed at and put down all these years is true, all too true. Another man across from him, pumping unleaded into his van, looks up—and drops the nozzle. It's Jesus. He's really come back. And immediately he knows that the wait for his Friend has been worth it.

One taken, the other left behind. One awake, the other sleeping.

What's the Second Coming going to be for you? It matters whether you are prepared for that surprise of a lifetime. It's one of the things that matters most.

Please don't be caught sleeping on that most important date in history. Please take responsibility for your own spiritual state right now. Please don't assume someone else can take care of it. Don't be swallowed up by the routine. Make God a priority in your life right now. Establish a friendship with Jesus Christ, right now.

You've got to decide to do it. You've got to allow God to get into your heart and into your life. If you don't decide, you'll end up sleeping, and you'll wake up to the most terrifying surprise of your lifetime.

It's so much better to wake up now. It's so much better to acknowledge what's most important now—rather than later when it's too late. So let's take that step right now.

Which Resurrection?

It was one of the last imposing ceremonies of the Soviet Empire: the funeral of Leonid Brezhnev. The generals were all there. The escort of smart-stepping soldiers. The display of military hardware. The banners and flags.

Everything was in place to show the world how this Communist regime could honor its head of state. Everything was staged to give the impression that the Soviet Union would go on forever. Everything conformed to the script—except for one small gesture.

It happened when Brezhnev's widow walked up to the imposing coffin. She paused a moment. And then she leaned forward and made the sign of the cross on her husband's chest.

Strong armies and ideology are one thing. But when it comes to hope beyond the grave—we have to look somewhere else.

People are looking in all kinds of places these days—for hope beyond the grave.

They're looking at Eastern religions. They're thinking that maybe becoming one with the cosmos offers a way out. Maybe reincarnation is the answer.

They're looking into the occult. Maybe contact with the dead will show us something about the "other side."

They're looking at science. Cryogenics seems to offer hope for some—freezing our bodies until science comes up with a way for us to live forever.

And they're looking, above all, at "near death experiences." These, more than anything else, seem to offer us a peek at life beyond the grave. People want some personal reassurance about that final journey. And more and more individuals these days are returning from "near death experiences," NDEs, to give us first-hand accounts.

Betty Eadie says she went to heaven and back during an NDE. She met Jesus and received many new teachings from Him. That is what she claimed, anyway, in her 1992 book *Embraced by the Light*. Plenty of people wanted to know what Betty saw up there. Her book stayed on the *New York Times* bestseller lists for a year and a half.

Betty wrote that she encountered Jesus as a benevolent being of light. Sometimes she couldn't tell where her "light" stopped and His began. Betty described a very loving Jesus who made her feel worthy to be with Him and embrace Him.

This part of her story fits the picture of Christ we get in the New Testament. But Betty had several other things to say which don't. For example, this woman concluded, based on her "near death experience" that Jesus is a being completely separate from the Father.

She also concluded that she should stop regretting past deeds because Jesus would do nothing to offend her.

She concluded that humans are not sinful creatures by nature.

That human "spirit beings" assisted God at Creation.

And that, despite appearances, there's really no tragedy in this world.

Now, Betty Eadie's NDE happened nearly 20 years before her book was published. She refuses to release her medical records and says that the physician in charge when she almost died has since passed away.

There's not a lot we can check about what really happened to Betty. But we *can* check on her reports of what Jesus told her. And that is what raises questions. Because some of the "teaching" she received seems much closer to NDE talk than to the Bible. That is, it fits other messages people have supposedly received through NDEs than it does the teaching of Scripture.

Lots of people have been claiming to bring the world new truth in this way, through near death experiences. In *Saved by the Light*, Dannion Brinkley claimed to share mysterious counsel he'd received from 13 luminous beings. That book became a big seller too. We've also had *Life After Life, Recollections of Death,* and *Closer To The Light.*

All these claims of a blissful experience on "the other side" have created what one researcher calls "the religion of the resuscitated." In this religion there's no fear of divine judgment. There's no problem with sin, no need of salvation. You just flow into the light and love.

In one book, called *Heading Toward Omega*, a heavenly being who appears during an NDE, consoles an anxious woman with these words "there are no sins."

The "religion of the resuscitated" doesn't focus on God so much as it does on the unlimited potential of humans. Betty Eadie talks of experiencing omniscience during her NDE, and she claims that her thoughts now have "tremendous power" to create reality. She also affirms that she was there at Creation as a preincarnate spirit and that her soul progresses eternally. These are beliefs that seem to come from her background as a Mormon.

Douglas Groothuis, writing in *Christianity Today*, concluded that these NDE phenomena often conform to New Age beliefs: Once we're freed from the fear of death and awaken to our own power, human beings can enter a glorious new consciousness.

In other words, the "religion of the resuscitated" puts

everyone in the same boat when they cross the river to the other side. There's no question of a judgment, no question of personal accountability. We're all headed for the same afterlife. It's sort of a value-free eternity. It's just one nice big pool of light up there somewhere.

May I suggest that there's much more to the afterlife than what "near death experiences" are telling us? There's a vitally important truth that's being overlooked—and even many Christians have overlooked it.

Now, let's see what the Bible has to say about facing the afterlife. This may come as a surprise, but Scripture actually speaks, not of one resurrection at the end of the age, but of TWO. That's right, there are *two* resurrections—two vastly different resurrections. In fact, they are resurrections headed in opposite directions, if you can conceive of such a thing. So it makes all the difference in the world which resurrection we experience.

Let's take a look at the first one the Bible talks about. This one takes place in a spectacular setting. Paul describes it in 1 Thessalonians: "For the Lord Himself will descend from heaven with a shout, with the voice of an archangel, and with the trumpet of God. And the dead in Christ will rise first. Then we who are alive and remain shall be caught up together with them in the clouds to meet the Lord in the air. And thus we shall always be with the Lord" (1 Thessalonians 4:16, 17, NKJV).

The dead in Christ will rise first. This is the first resurrection. It takes place at the second coming of Jesus Christ. The Bible tells us that Jesus is going to descend from heaven one day, the same Jesus who ministered in Galilee 2000 years ago. The kingdom of God will suddenly swoop down on earth.

And at that time, those who are *in Christ*, those who've developed a relationship with Him, will awaken to a glorious eternity with Jesus. That trumpet of God pierces down into the tomb. The same Creator who fashioned life on this planet goes to work again, turning skeletons into living human beings, recreating lost minds, lost personalities. And then the resurrected join those believers who are still living and ascend toward heaven with Christ.

That incredible journey begins, for all believers, living or dead, with a dramatic transformation.

Paul describes exactly what will happen to all those faithful to Christ in 1 Corinthians: "We will not all sleep, but we will all be changed—in a flash, in the twinkling of an eye, at the last trumpet. For the trumpet will sound, the dead will be raised imperishable, and we will be changed" (1 Corinthians 15:51-52, NIV).

Paul tells us that this is when believers are given immortality, this is when death is swallowed up in victory. Those who are IN CHRIST receive perfect new bodies, new hearts and minds. No sickness, no weakness, no decay will ever touch us again.

In the book of Philippians, Paul further explains what awaits those who eagerly wait for their Saviour, those whose citizenship is in heaven. He says, in Philippians, that Jesus Christ: "Will transform our lowly body that it may be conformed to His glorious body" (Philippians 3:21, NKJV).

Believers are going to have a very real life with Jesus in a very real body, a glorious body. That's what happens in the first resurrection, the resurrection to eternal life.

But Paul is also very clear about another event, a very different event: the second resurrection. It takes place a thousand years after the first resurrection. In other words, after the millennium when the righteous are in heaven with Christ. It is called a resurrection of condemnation when all the wicked are confronted with judgment.

Revelation 20 tells us about this: "The sea gave up the dead that were in it, and death and Hades gave up the dead that were in them, and each person was judged according to what he had done. If anyone's name was not found written in the book of life, he was thrown into the lake of fire" (Revelation 20:13, 15, NIV).

This is earth's final tragedy, an awakening that does not awaken, a rising from sleep that only leads to eternal slumber. It is difficult for us to imagine the sense of loss of those who look at God in all His glory and realize that they will never, never be a part of life with Him in heaven. They will miss out on eternity! What inexpressible anguish that thought must bring. No wonder Scripture describes it as a time when there will be weeping and gnashing of teeth.

Two resurrections. Two destinies. Two vastly different eternities.

But here's the important point. The second resurrection is entirely avoidable, no one has to stumble into that lake of fire, no one has to experience eternal annihilation.

It's avoidable because of what God has done. The Father isn't just some indifferent judge sitting up on His throne, sending this one to one fate, that one to another. He doesn't arbitrarily determine human destinies. No, the Father is very active in trying to rescue us from the wrong destiny.

Look at His appeal in Ezekiel. This is God Himself speaking through the prophet: "Repent! Turn away from all your offenses; then sin will not be your downfall. Rid yourselves of all the offenses you have committed, and get a new heart and a new spirit. Why will you die? . . . I take no pleasure in the death of anyone, declares the Sovereign Lord. Repent and live!" (Ezekiel 18:30-32, NIV).

Two resurrections set human beings off in opposite directions. But God's attitude is: No one needs to die! Why will you die? Repent and live!

If we take responsibility for our offenses before God, if we receive the pardon that Christ offers from the Cross, if we repent—then we can be assured of coming up in the first resurrection.

This is the promise that Christ makes in the book of

Revelation: "He who overcomes shall not be hurt by the second death" (Revelation 2:11, NKJV).

We can all escape the finality of the second death. We can all be overcomers. Why? Because as Scripture tells us, we overcome by the blood of the Lamb. We overcome because Christ has defeated sin and the power of evil on the cross. We overcome because we find salvation and acceptance through the sacrifice Jesus made. That's how we find eternal life.

Do you see that the Bible offers every human being great hope, wonderful hope? This is very different from the vague hope offered by "near death experiences" and the "religion of the resuscitated." What the Bible shows us is more than just a pool of light. It's real life with a real God; it's face-to-face encounters; it's paradise with Christ.

The hope of Scripture isn't "value free." No, it takes us seriously as moral beings, as responsible human beings. The hope of Scripture calls us to account. The hope of Scripture asks us to deal honestly with sin. The hope of Scripture goes through the Cross! That's the big difference.

That's why Leonid Brezhnev's widow made that sign of the cross on her husband's chest. In the midst of all the pomp and circumstance of the Soviet Empire, she had to go back to the hope offered by a carpenter from Nazareth.

Her gesture flew in the face of the atheistic regime that surrounded her. But she had to cling to something more solid, Someone more solid than anything communism could offer.

We can have confidence in an afterlife because we can have confidence in Jesus. Through Jesus we can confidently deal with guilt. We can be assured of our acceptance before a holy God. We can have confidence in a personal afterlife because we can have confidence in our identity and security in Christ.

That's the kind of hope we need. That's a hope we can

cling to. That's a hope that will get us through the roughest times.

Let me tell you about a few people who had to face death in the most trying of circumstances.

In China during the Boxer uprising, August of 1900, a young mother and missionary, Lizzie Atwater, had to face the prospect of a brutal death at the hands of Boxer fanatics who had sworn vengeance on all foreigners. She had to wait in agonizing suspense as the bands of marauders closed in on her compound. And she waited, clutching a baby to her breast.

But in this time of terror, Lizzie found a way to hope. This is what she wrote to her sister and her family shortly before her death:

"I long for a sight of your dear faces, but I fear we shall not meet on earth. I am preparing for the end very quietly and calmly. The Lord is wonderfully near, and He will not fail me. I was very restless and excited while there seemed a chance of life, but God has taken away that feeling, and now I just pray for grace to meet the terrible end bravely. The pain will soon be over, and oh the sweetness of the welcome above!"

In Ecuador, January 1956, Roj Youderian was killed while trying to share the gospel with Auca Indians in the jungle.

Days after his body was found, Roj's wife, Barbara, wrote this in her private journal: "God gave me this verse in Psalm 48 two days ago: 'For this is God, Our God forever and ever; He will be our guide Even to death.' [Psalm 48:14, NKJV].

"I wrote a letter to the mission family, trying to explain the peace I have."

In the Belgian Congo, September of 1956, missionary Lois Carlson had to face her husband's death listening to the static from a short-wave radio. Dr. Paul Carlson's hospital had been overrun by Simba nationalists.

Once in awhile, he could sneak out a brief message on the shortwave. Lois caught this sentence, "Where I go from here I know not, only that it will be with Him."

Days later, another message: "I know I'm ready to meet my Lord, but my thought for you makes this more difficult. I trust that I might be a witness for Christ."

When they found Dr. Carlson's body, slain at the hospital, there was a New Testament in his jacket pocket. In its pages, the doctor had written the date—it was the day before he was shot—and he'd penned a single word: "Peace."

Peace in the face of the worst of circumstances. Peace in the face of death. That only happens when people have a profound sense of security, a profound sense of trust in the One who will be with them in the end.

People experience peace who know which resurrection awaits them. They know that they are going to awaken to see Jesus coming through the clouds, lighting up the sky. They know that they will be transformed. They know that they will never again experience heartache and pain and death. They know that they will spend eternity with Jesus.

Do you have that assurance? Or are you just hoping to drift into some vague afterlife? Do you know whose hand will pull you through? Or are you just hoping to end up in some pool of light somewhere?

God wants you to live. He had gone to great lengths to make the second resurrection, the resurrection of condemnation—avoidable. But you have to take a step away from that resurrection—and to the other. You need to respond to God's call to repent and believe. You need to take your relationship with Him seriously.

Which is it going to be for you? Eternal life or a never-ending death? Which resurrection are you going to choose?